The Widow's Lovers

The Widow's Lovers

Poems on

Longing, Loving and Letting Go

by

Pamela Brothers Denyes

© 2022 Pamela Brothers Denyes. All rights reserved.
This material may not be reproduced in any form, published,
reprinted, recorded, performed, broadcast,
rewritten or redistributed without
the explicit permission of Pamela Brothers Denyes.
All such actions are strictly prohibited by law.

Cover design by Shay Culligan
Cover image by Vika Fleysher (on Unsplash)
Author photo by Pamela Brothers Denyes

ISBN: 978-1-63980-218-0

Kelsay Books
502 South 1040 East, A-119
American Fork, Utah 84003
Kelsaybooks.com

For the ones
who beckoned me
back to love

Acknowledgments

Grateful acknowledgements are given to the following literary journals and anthologies where some of these poems have been published or will soon appear:

Black Moon Magazine: "Magician"

Fauxmoir Literary Magazine: "Searching Remembered Rooms"

I Have a Dream: "Safe in My Running"

Journal of the Blue Ridge Writers: "First Impression," "From Where We Awaken," "Interlude," "Strength of a Wish"

Journal of the Virginia Writers Club, Spring 2022: "Cosmic Giggle"

Journal of the Virginia Writers Club, Summer 2021: "Arid Surface"

MindFull Magazine: "Carry You with Me," "Ready"

Shakespeare of Today: "Sonnet for a New Life"

Tangled Locks Journal: "A Poet's Online Dating Profile"

The Black Haven: "Prisoner"

The Right Mistakes: "Acceptably Beautiful," "Casting Stones," "de·sire," "For a Hand in Mine," "The Mystery"

Virginia Bards Central Review: "Find Me the Moonflower"

I offer grateful thanks to Joe in Pittsburgh, my first poetry challenge partner. Thanks, also, to Latorial Faison for being my first established poet friend and for bolstering my newfound desire to be a writer.

Contents

Releasing the Grief	13
Carry You with Me	14
Sonnet for a New Life	15
Angry Puckered Pout	16
Ready	17
For a Hand in Mine	18
Fair Warning	19
de·sire	20
Find Me the Moonflower	21
The Mystery	22
Infinite Lust	23
Somebody Else's Footprints	24
Your Unequal Replacement	25
From Where We Awaken	26
Ancient Photos	27
A Poet's Online Dating Profile	28
Only Do Lunch	30
Arid Surface	31
The Complicated One	32
Sunrise—Sunset—Sunrise	33
Cosmic Giggle	34
Acceptably Beautiful	35
The Videos	36
First Impression	37
an·ti·ci·pa·tion	38
New	39
The Monet	40
Something about You	41
Only You	42
If You Knew	43
Leap Day 2016	44
I Will Not Go	45
Like It's No Big Deal	46

Other People's Love Poems	47
Letter from a Pathological Liar, 1967	48
Still Forever	49
end·ing	50
Mid-winter Moonlight	51
Surprised	52
Love Never Spoken	53
Your Disguises	54
Interlude	55
Stealing My Last First Kiss	56
Someone Like Me	57
Before You Find Me	58
Safe in My Running	59
Filing Away the Secrets	60
Kisses That Fed Us	61
Grasping for the Fog	62
A Share of You	63
Floating Peace	64
fas·ci·nate	65
Magician	66
Spilling Away	67
Unpacking a Year	68
Separating the Bleeding Things	69
Strength of a Wish	70
Meet for Coffee	71
Walls	72
Prisoner	73
Casting Stones	74
I Don't Even Ask	75
Count the Stars	76
Did You Notice?	77
Searching Remembered Rooms	78
Companionship	79

Spending My One Life	80
The First One After	81
Love Is	82
Just Once More	83

Releasing the Grief

In my grief, I ran away. Oh, friends were near, but I was distant, unaware of my purpose, or any design for carrying on without my mate. Eighteen years of devotion, six harrowing months of decay, ninety days of disbelief and disorientation, were followed by ten days of cruising France's waterways, hoping a faraway full emotional upheaval could rinse away the anguish, could press me forward to a new life without my greatest love. Certainly, the golden aura of Provence, that persistent sunlight, would bake the grief out of me, leaving only the sweet love. Standing on the bow as the ship slipped down the Rhône, wind blowing tears over my shoulder, the grief left me, and I was released.

Carry You with Me

I will not carry the astounding
grief of your illness, your sad
passing from our life together.
It is released, vanquished
from the storehouse of my
humble hopeful heart.

As you have passed beyond
the veil and I have not,
so every together-thought,
the travel plans, family dreams
yet have life to go forward,
if I will cease to grieve you.

Yes, I will wish you were here,
name your name in love always,
remember you to family,
to friends who treasured you
in your one magnificent life,
and forever carry you with me.

Sonnet for a New Life

I have released everything old
To see what may be left.
Will former joys soon fade away,
This moment feel bereft?

Spin and spin, this mind of mine,
Till you settle with new peace,
In a tranquil state that feels to you
Like love can never cease,

As though you only turned a cheek
To see that dear face anew,
And found yourself again beside
That love you recent knew.

Drift, drift away, oh heart forlorn,
To know your fulsome joy reborn!

Angry Puckered Pout

In the dream, I spent all day next door at the young neighbor's, with the new baby. I wandered over to check on her and stayed during a sudden crazy-for-spring snowstorm, complete with thunder and lightning, hail hitting our cars, a power outage, feet of snow, trouble with baby latching on, her older child jealously acting out, a nagging sense I had to be somewhere, and me barefoot.

    Nonsense.

I scampered home barefooted and there you were, conducting a meeting at the kitchen table with your whole face wrinkled into an angry puckered pout. Ladies wandering the house told me how happy they were that we were finally getting married, which you had not told me yet. I thought, wow, one day away in all these years, he's horribly upset and *now* he's ready to marry?

    Crazy, huh?

Today it's been nine years since you died. When I awoke, I realized that I had forgotten your angry puckered pout, how you seemed able to combine all of your feelings on your face at one time—you are so precious, you hurt me terribly, I love you, how can I forgive you—all over your eyes and mouth. That's when I understood that you hadn't shown me that face in the last few years of our marriage . . .

    and I cried again.

Ready

Don't wait to stretch out
into the life you still have.
Time flies; opportunity fades.

It won't wait for you
to catch up when you think
you're ready.

You may move away
or stay right where you are,
but home will never be the same.

Sleep or not, you will have dreams,
good and bad, and you will
see your beloved again there.

You made a fine life before;
you can do it again.
Don't wait to be ready.

For a Hand in Mine

I would fly to the moon
To capture her moon beams,

Maybe go on through the luminous
Universe collecting stardust for you,

Swim the teeming seas searching
For a just-right beach for love-making,

Sleep together in Tut's pyramid to hear
Our loving words echo in ancient chambers,

Ride the back of a she-elephant across
The Alps to meet you in Rome,

Build a beautiful love-trap apartment
In Paris to intrigue and draw you in,

Become a master painter so I can
Give eternity to your dynamism,

Choose you every single day,
Loving, uplifting and holding your hand.

Fair Warning

Fair warning: I write poetry.
You and your life are going to be
in a poem, if you're lucky, if
you make any impression at all.

My dates dance through my poems
these last ten years, but it's possible
that I won't write about you at all.
This fate is not to be desired.

My readers will expect a poem, and if
there are none about you, will condemn
you to the shameful basement
of suitors who failed to impress.

de·sire

> : to long for, wish for or hope for
> some person or thing not yet
> in one's possession

It seeps away and flows
down to the basement
where I store boxed up
resentment, anger,
all my old feelings.

It dreams quietly there
in the dark underground,
waiting to wrap me like
a warm blanket when I open
the door and turn on the light.

When aroused, sleepy desire
remembers only the good parts
of loving another, without clinging
tightly to the difficult bits
or the inconsolable pain.

Find Me the Moonflower

Find me the fragrance of the moonflower
which blooms in the dark lonely midnight,
whose delicate scent is so rare and pure, to
prove you know the value of what you seek.

Bring to me meat that never breathed,
but nourishes body, mind and soul.
Give me the bow that does not destroy
any other being in the quest for peace.

Know me deeply from the energy you feel.
Focus only on that eternal beauty which
breathes its life through me, creating all
that I am in this world.

Find me the fragrance of the moonflower,
here for just one luscious night at a time,
to give her fragrant expression of life
to the one who respects her truth.

The Mystery

What a mystery it is that love opens us again and again!
Though combat scars still bleed, we seek another, better
chance to pour ourselves fully into loving another being.

Hurt places heal, bruised hearts feel stronger rhythm,
pumping sweet blind hope through still gaping wounds
from previous battles, and we feel love again.

This pulsing red hope, coursing through battle-worn
bodies, crosses the blood-brain barrier like no drug
ever will, selectively erasing painful lessons and errors.

So new love appears not as a war but as a tasty mystery,
a bright joyful expedition of unexplored territory,
rich with exciting possibilities.

Pressing on toward precious rewards in a passionate
heart-driven conquest, in spite of ourselves
we are opened by love once again.

Infinite Lust

I usually fall
for the one
who's looking
straight
into the camera,

with an impish grin,
always dressed
only in blues
that flatter him,
holding a guitar

between his thighs
like a beautiful woman,
hugging it
with strong legs
and infinite lust.

Somebody Else's Footprints

It doesn't hold me back anymore,
but it haunts me, that deeply primal
nesting need, an interior driving force
to craft a life that two can share.

Oh, it rises, clutching for my throat,
as I reread my happy-sad-angry-sorry
notes about pairing and unpairing
and pairing again.

Sometimes a fevered dream pulls me
into deep water, choking, and I fear
I will drown without—who?
Escaping, I rise alone, gulping for life.

A long overdue wave of honesty
washes me onto a restless shore.
I weep quietly as it washes away
somebody else's footprints.

Your Unequal Replacement

Another winter solstice
sparkles in crisp air.
Wood smoke scents my jacket.

December offers only dry
lifeless leaves, whirling
in whispering brown circles.

It's another low-key day,
so thoughts turn to you, gone
now more than seven years.

With the sun setting early,
it will be a bone-cold night.
I don't want to leave the house,

though somewhere out there
your unequal replacement
is looking for me.

From Where We Awaken

    For "Just Steve"

"Be true to your heart,"
he writes 53 years later.

        For me, it was a sleepy summer dream,
        foolish youth and false investment.

"Time, choices, effort . . . Did I
try too hard, not enough?"

        Such is ever the heartbreaking
        paradox of slumberous passion.

"Least resistance leads
to temporary success . . ."

        What can we do with safely boxed away
        memories, the time and distance?

"There was a huge cost . . .
my life's course would be so different."

        So we move on
        from where we awaken.

Ancient Photos

Deep inside I suppose I am still the laughing girl,
the same carefree long-blonde singer who drew you in,
with an attraction lasting fifty-three years, so far.

But now I am more me than her, and you're clearly
only interested in fifteen-year-old me. Take her.

Honestly, she is not half the amazing woman
I have become, which you will never know
because you won't look past the ancient photos.

A Poet's Online Dating Profile

I smell like ginger, apples and caramel, and often garlic.
My voice is a magnolia blowing in a sea breeze.

I have hungry hands that demand to be held.
My tiny ears connect to my heart, not my brain.

I am soft and warm, except in the hurt places, where
I am dangerously sharp and wince at allowing newcomers.

My lips are raspberries with lemon zest.
My green-blue ocean eyes can rinse a soul clean.

I am a Water Dragon, born on the cusp of Virgo and Libra,
with the best and worst tendencies of both.

My mind is wordy, argues with me about what I want,
and is hard to put to bed, like a four-year-old.

I have a quirky smile with a mind of its own.
My body glides magnetically to a body I love.

I feel deeply and often give too much of me away.
My heart lives on my sleeve; tears may run down my arm.

I enjoy an orderly space and hate to clean; I do it anyway.
My days are colorful, creative and conscientious.

My sons and grandkids are precious like water to me.
A vivid imagination gives me more life than I can ever live.

I can hide like a bandit and run away from what scares me,
and sometimes what scares me is actually good for me.

I struggle to remember that self-doubt is not a stop sign.
I must take a walk to lose a difficult mood or simple anger.

I am a positive-minded Pollyanna, with Mary Poppins'
practical magic for good measure.

My emotions rule my body; I keep them happy and healthy.
I light up like Christmas when the right person walks in.

My life is busy, challenging, loving, giving, rarely boring,
and I can feel it beginning to slow down.

Only Do Lunch

Girlfriends said, "Try online dating, but only do lunch. That's how I found . . ." "a husband," "a handsome, successful boyfriend," or at least "a good time."

> What an eye-opening experience, to discover
> how utterly naïve I am at my advanced age!

At lunch with the first guy, we share our mutual love of music and travel, then he reveals that his semi-annual journeys were for his eight elective cosmetic surgeries. Umm, no.

During number two's lunch, after texts and phone calls, the interesting PhD historian reveals that he's seeking a "conjugal" secondary girlfriend in my city. Hell, no!

> What a foolish mealtime quest, unlikely to uncover
> a just-right match for my quirky artsy lifestyle.

One more try: nice guy meets me for dinner, and immediately afterwards, posts a goodbye to online dating, he's "found the one." He courts, I succumb. All is good until he reveals he is sworn never to love any other woman than his fifteen-years-dead wife.

> Nah, I don't need this; I'll stick to lunching
> with my girlfriends!

Arid Surface

Floating terra cotta hills against
impossibly blue skies.

Adobe buildings—red, brown, tan—
bounded by succulent blooming cacti.

Trails so chokingly dusty a kerchief
covers my nose and mouth.

Arroyos crackled dry, I easily cross,
following the path of energy

That rises and resonates
from the earth's roiling core.

It pulls me deeper into it, into myself,
as I climb each sunset-pink hillside.

It amplifies feelings I brought with me
to this sacred Sedona mountain:

Red-chili emotions buried shallow,
just beneath my own arid surface.

The Complicated One

"Iris," I said, when he asked my favorite flower,
though I could not say why. "Truly, I love them all,"
I said, blushing, "but if I must choose, I'll say iris."

A complicated blue-purple, with high standards,
she stretches taller than others, not in judgment
but striving for her own individual perfection.

The patient, most observant ones will see meticulous
details in her delicate beauty, revealed over time,
not overnight, painting every petal with surprises.

Speak to her intelligent heart with your mind.
Prove that you, too, have a higher perspective,
that you live with self-understanding.

She will open in joy to you.

Sunrise—Sunset—Sunrise

A salty almond wakes my taste buds,
tired of tasteless, weary of home cooking,
desiring intricate dishes with sunrise spices
cooked by a very fine chef.

Cool Chardonnay rinses salt from my tongue,
sudden sunlight in my mouth. This season
I taste fine wines with a new friend,
visiting spring-green wineries at sunset.

Yes, please—come close. Let me taste the wine
from your lips. Share some of you with me.
My tongue is salt but soon you will know
my sunrise lips are honey and fire.

Cosmic Giggle

The sun spirits its way through your fog.
You imagine my laughter like tingsha bells,
though you have not heard it yet.

My one-dimensional Mona Lisa-smile gazes
invitingly at you from the photo, without
the honest intrusion of physical dimension.

Like a faint cosmic giggle, tingsha bells
bring your thoughts to center. Your own
perception of me connects with you there,

and I laugh.

Acceptably Beautiful

Acceptably beautiful . . .
what a loaded phrase!

Hours spent, money invested
in a shallow, mercurial image,
hiding the truth of a person,
washing away the reality,

is not what I want for me, nor
what you should ask of me.
As you reach for my hand,
only the love in me shines—

acceptably beautiful.

The Videos

You have videos online.
I heard your voice,
saw you move your body.

We haven't met yet,
and your Georgia accent
has already won me.

Will you bear-hug me
today when we meet?
Will conversation flow?

You're fitting me in,
rushing from rehearsal,
told me you'll be late.

Take your time;
I won't be alone.
You have videos online.

First Impression

He smiled as he recognized me, maybe a little prettier in person. Sauntering to our table like a bear on two legs, his smile won me right away. I say that about all smiling faces, don't I? I had that "haven't I met you before" feeling that not all smiling faces bring. He looked tired, a sacrifice to be here with me now.

We lunched, then went into the museum. He arranged a private tour of the Impressionist Gallery—appropriate for our first impression day, I thought. Walking with this tall bear-man, I longed to hold his expressive long-fingered hand, to be very close as we toured Sisley, Cassatt, Monet—small collection but fine art.

When the docent left us, my new bear-friend moved closer, reaching for my hand with his fine, tree-strong fingers. Pulling it to his whispering lips, he kissed each of my fingers before our hands disappeared into his cavernous coat pocket.

an·ti·ci·pa·tion

: the act of looking forward to a
pleasurable experience; visualization
of a future event or state

You will be here today, so I
dust and polish,
light a candle,
put away everything
except my true nature.

I will watch out for
bumbles and stumbles,
foolish words and giggles,
choices low and high,
shallow breathing.

I'm smiling my best
"I'm still here" smile.
What I wear doesn't matter;
who I am does. Still,
I spray on my sexiest perfume.

You are ringing the bell.
Everything is done.
We can just explore
with anticipation.
Take a deep breath.

New

You brought me flowers from your garden;
I cooked you dinner in my style.
Looks like the age-old pattern for courting,
But for us, it is new.

I reach for your fits-like-a-glove hand;
You pull me in close and tight.
So many love stories have begun like this,
But for us, it is new.

You survived her long life-robbing battle;
I fought his quick death just half a year.
We are not the first to start over after,
But for us, it is new.

If our hearts mate for life, it must be true,
That we'll carry their love forward with us,
Always honoring who they were in our past,
But for us, it is new.

The Monet

A promising lover took my hand
To lead me up his stairwell.
Tender words were spoken soft
As I lost all thoughts of farewell.

Arriving in that simple space
I saw preparations he had made.
Just for me, a new Monet,
Above his old bed was displayed.

To place my favorite painter's work
Above his rose-strewn bed
Woke me to the lover he might be,
Holding both my heart and head.

Amazed, my own soft kisses rose
To meet his fevered pitch.
Passion bloomed in the gentle man
As we tore off every stitch.

Hand in hand we danced a bit,
Then moved as one for a while.
First time was not perfection,
Though the Monet gave it style.

But in the dark and quiet
Of that passionate moonlit night
One hand reached out for the other,
Then two bodies found delight.

Alas, I cannot say this man
Loved me in just the right way,
But I'll remember his tenderness,
And, of course, his colorful Monet.

Something about You

He tossed his big-name business card
across the table, not really for a business venture.
Impish brown eyes asked, "Didn't I used to know you?"

No, we were not ready when we were younger,
but maybe we would enjoy each other now.
Suddenly he grabbed me, danced me around,

pulled me close, my back against his chest,
arms around my shoulders in a sweetheart squeeze.
Laughing, I turned my face up to a surprise kiss.

For those moments, we were a little more,
joined by the embrace, laughter in our eyes,
warmth of August-hot bodies touching.

Someone snapped our photo for social media.
As I walked away, I heard him chuckle,
"something about you!"

Only You

Never had a man create mixtapes for me
from his own vast collection of tunes,
telling me so much about himself.

No man ever insisted on holding my coat,
gently pulling my hair out from the collar,
opening my car door as a sign of honor.

Never had a man wrap me tenderly
in a warm blanket like a treasured present,
then bring my favorite wine.

No man has ever taken the long way home
just for me, knowing how much I enjoy
riding out one way and coming home another.

No man was ever so proud with me on his arm,
walking into every room grinning ear to ear.
Only you.

Now, what can I do for you?

If You Knew

What if you knew that I still
drive by your house because,
well,
you still live there?

What if you knew how many
poems I've written about you,
so far,
over these lost years?

What if you knew back then,
how much I cherished you?
Maybe
I didn't speak your language.

What if you knew I drove by today,
wrote you another poem, and
still
miss you like air?

Leap Day 2016

On January 1, 2016, after two years of break-ups and loving make-ups, I decided to ask you to commit yourself to me on February 29, Sadie Hawkins Day, when girls may ask. February winds blew in, cooling your heart. The sweetness drained away and again we marched toward break-up. My desire to ask you to marry melted like spring snow. When February 29 arrived, I was committed to you as a beloved friend, but knew that you could never choose me as I had chosen you. So I did not ask. We didn't know that it was your adult autism, blasting away at our relationship, doubt pressing us apart time and again. One final time, it pushed me away from you. Four long years have passed, with me pining for your hungry kisses, deep blue-hazel eyes, delicious sense of humor, playing music together, and most of all, your loving embrace. If I see you tomorrow, February 29, 2020, I will tell you what I almost did in 2016.

Or will I ask?

I Will Not Go

You will not go from my heart,
which aches for you again.
Memories pull, thoughts push me
in your direction.
I will not go.

I will not go, but I see you
watching me from across the room,
she who was once so devoted to you.
Disgusted by my new short haircut,
you will not come.

You will not come to my table,
dive again into my ocean eyes,
bringing the patchouli-on-you scent
you know that I still crave.
I will not come.

I will not come into your arms lightly,
as I have over and over again,
dancing through the years,
flirting, following, falling.
You will not go.

You will not go until our lives are done.
No more loving, no more expectations,
time simply completed for someone.
Even then, as life drains from you or me,
I will not go.

Like It's No Big Deal

I've been acting like it's no big deal,
adding a new lover into my life,
but at our age, it is!

I've grown to be a curmudgeon,
ungracefully intolerant of others'
foolishness. I don't even hide it.

I rarely accept excessive anything,
especially if it undeniably impairs health
or life in the real world.

I'll have you read old poems, written
around other suitors' faults and foibles,
and consider you fairly warned.

Trying to be open with you, I will outline
the many quirks of my old-lady body
before you make love to me.

And sleep? I'm not sure I can sleep
with someone else in the bed again,
maybe a king bed. I roll all night.

If, in spite of all this, we find new love,
I will be a devoted partner and friend,
rising above the warnings.

Other People's Love Poems

Some writers raise my fire, make me crave
that poet alone; others do not.

What fun it is to choose whose love poems
move me, best heighten my passion,

driving my breath in a shallow pattern
until I quiver with the words.

Letter from a Pathological Liar, 1967

Dear Steve,

    We plan to come up to the game on November 2. It might be touchy for Pam 'cause she's fond of this boy from USC. I like him, too, but not as much as you!

    Don't worry about those other boys. She's just having a good time right now, but YOU are still my favorite!

    I expect we'll bring her home from the hospital in a few days. She got more flowers this afternoon, but none as lovely as yours!

    You know, it doesn't hurt at all, to have the girl's Mother in YOUR corner!

    If you EVER tell Pam I told you all this, I'll swear you are a pathological liar!

            Luv you,
                Mrs. B

Still Forever

Numbness presses down my regret,
stubbornly occupying brain cells.

Brain cells hold memories: I was afraid
to hold you—though I loved you.

Loved you before we had grown-up cares,
never understanding you'd love this long.

This long loving is your monument
to what you meant by love.

By love you meant forever,
and it is now still forever.

end·ing

> : conclusion, cessation, closure or
> discontinuance of a course of action

Rip it away.
Sometimes the best thing to do

is turn the page and begin again.
It's quick. It's not painless,

but it's over. There's a scary
freedom in ripping away

your own bloodied bandage
that has protected the wound

all this time. Hard to be sure
the bleeding won't start up again,

but now you know how
not to die over it.

Mid-winter Moonlight

Our kisses are always passion-filled
body blocks, full and open, sometimes
knocking me to my knees.

In a nightcap embrace, in your tiny kitchen,
middle of the night, after a hot concert date,
the radio plays slow, sexy all-night jazz.

Wrapping your arms around me, you laugh
as you pull off my shirt. I tease and dance,
unbuttoning your jeans, which fall with a thud

to the ancient jute-covered linoleum.
My breast in your hand, we dance, heat rises,
clothing flies. We're laughing, singing, kissing,

almost bare in the white-cold mid-winter
moonlight, sparkling like crisp frost
through your tiny kitchen's window.

Surprised

Startled to see you, I woke up gasping,
quilted in the warmth of sound sleep,
instantly wanting to call you.

I still need to ask if you're okay,
to know if you need me there.

When you show up in a dream,
or some sudden urgent memory,
it's like licking an envelope:

I'm always surprised by the taste
but not that the glue is there.

Love Never Spoken

You have ruined me for anyone else.

Now I measure them all
against the height and breadth
of love never spoken aloud,

by the words of a mind and heart
whose face I will never kiss,
except with words.

It is a passion we forged in absentia,
without one physical moment
to express the pleasure.

Your Disguises

Searching for your one
honest face,

I find only tweets, retweets
and hashtags,

disguises for the fullness
of a man who hides

like the reticent god particle,
skating along the eightfold path.

Interlude

Excitement builds as the orchestra begins
the introduction to Rossini's Cinderella,
familiar but not tired, light but not frivolous.
I watch bear-strong fingers make sweet
love to your dark curvy double bass,
enjoying the plush seat you arranged after you
said that you don't think of me as "a date."

Your bass delights at your touch, singing her
deep alto notes for your pleasure and mine.
I am lost in the beauty of the music and you.
When you carefully lay her aside to leave
the pit, I watch you, lumbering like a stiff
sleepy bear to find your new friend again
for the few moments of the interlude.

Because you told me where to find you,
I slip from my second-row aisle seat and,
like a sacred treasure hunt through
labyrinthine back halls, search for you,
sniffing for bear essence, that energy,
your full fine frame, and I find you waiting,
exactly where you chose to be found.

Your bear hug greets me, holds me longer
than before. Luminous hazel eyes gaze
into mine for one immeasurable moment.
Long fret fingers slide down my cheek,
lift my face to meet your lips in a hungry
first kiss that says clearly to me,
"I changed my mind."

Stealing My Last First Kiss

Middle of a week-long black quiet night, alone,
I am hot then achingly cold, lost, lonely in the shadows,
like waiting for someone to die.

My brain clatters on, a painted circus train, full
of wild animals, rattling across dusty Kansas, noisy,
hungry and over-heating. I have something to decide.

No, the choice is already made. I'll tell him today.
He won't be surprised. It must be the only reason
such a handsome man has no mate at his age. Still,

it saddens me and I am cold-steel numb, like waiting
for the hearse to arrive, angry at him for making this
long mistake: his lifestyle is foolish and deadening.

Pushing him away this early is safe, sane and sensible,
but now I feel crazy as I watch him disappear, lumbering
down my stairs, stealing my last first kiss.

Someone Like Me

It's something I don't talk about,
unless I am asked directly, then
I am cautious in revealing
this seemingly still uncommon thing.

I didn't tell you either, at first.
Strange to think of it now, but clearly
you must have seen me as nice, kind,
like you in all things that mattered.

Perhaps you'd never met someone like me,
to whom you were attracted so strongly.
You could not expect my hidden secret,
until I revealed it and ran from your caress.

I have no remorse over my difference,
but if we had continued a loving path,
how would you, anchored in strong faith,
live happily with one who does not believe?

Before You Find Me

"Say everything . . ." you texted,
after I had clearly spent five minutes
typing a long note to you,
only to erase it.

"Please."

But I cannot say everything
to you right now, maybe never.

You are still so deeply connected
to your late wife that it is too early,
currently unthinkable to pull you
into my arms, my bed, my heart.

Everything I write feels thinly hidden,
so I must erase some of it, carefully
crafting my widow's advice, while
gently backing down my feelings,

encouraging you to find yourself first,
before you find me.

Safe in My Running

I allowed our conversation to crawl up into my head,
so there you danced around in my dreams all night.

>Something you said or did scared me,
>challenged me so hard that I ran away from you.
>I took only my phone and car, and promptly
>got lost in higher-than-true hills around Richmond.
>
>I couldn't leave town until I picked up my suitcase,
>but in my fear and anger, I could not remember
>the location of the hotel and panicked. I found myself
>crying on a cliff, looking down at odd wide buildings.
>
>Just as I remembered that the reservation was still
>on my phone, you came up behind me, trying to assure
>me that everything would be okay, but I was still wary.
>How did you find me . . .?

As often happens in dreams, as soon as I
asked the question I knew the answer.

>You came after me.
>I had run away the very first time something got sticky
>between us, and you followed me, making sure I was
>safe in my running, to lead me out of my fear.
>
>No one has done that before.
>Ever.

A lump in my throat and cold tears on my cheek woke me,
with the certainty that something big has shifted.

Filing Away the Secrets

Where do you file away
the secrets of a friend,
ones no one can ever know
except you, the trusted one?

How do you carry the years
of untold stories, passions
that fulfilled your friend's soul
but could ostracize them forever?

What part of yourself do you
pack away with those secrets,
afraid to look too closely
or to let go completely?

Kisses That Fed Us

Of all the things I wish were still true,
top of the list is the way we first loved:

our eyes spoke all the words;
two bodies danced as one;

kisses fed us day and night;
hunger pulled us across a room;

you pressed the very breath
into my body with your kisses.

I wonder what you wish was still true.

Grasping for the Fog

So you saw him last night?
How did he sound? Happy, I hope?

Photo looks as handsome to me
as ever he did when we loved,

with a sexy question pausing
in those still-hungry eyes.

Sometimes I yearn for those
enjoyable bits and pieces of us

that never did actually add up
to a healthy relationship.

Even now I grasp hungrily
at this morning's fog, hoping

to hold a handful of low cloud,
then mourn the absence of it.

A Share of You

The *Fratres* you suggested
is playing, open and loud.

I feel you from your distance,
mentally reaching for me.

Listening for what you
wanted me to hear,

I am cool butter
sinking into a warm muffin,

nourished by the only part of you
that you share with me.

Floating Peace

The river's banks are full today,
water slipping gracefully past us.

Suddenly, you stop, slightly ahead of me.
I pause in silent expectation.

You're watching something in the shallows.
"Wait, look," says your lifted paddle,

crossed upon your lap in the kayak.
You see a green heron fishing, but I do not.

As your eyes admire the bird on the bank,
I savor your mirrored reflection.

Though the water ripples around your kayak,
your image floats in peace.

fas·ci·nate

    : to command the interest of; bewitch
      or hold spellbound, irresistible
    : from "fascinum," evil spell

The First Lover of my widowhood gripped me
against his orange car door in the dark-moon
parking lot of the rowdy bar where he drank away
his week's stinking disappointments every Friday night.

He bemused me with cloud-nine kisses, too-large hands
pulling me spellbound into his curious life, neither
fully adult nor child, transfixed by rare blue-hazel eyes,
eager as Niagara tumbling over the falls.

This charmed man-child teased out my best features
from darkened places where I had hidden them.
Ways we needed each other kept me in his grasp,
my purpose entangled with his happiness.

Alas, a child's mind seeks comfort if hard choice
beckons. Asking him to grow out of distraction,
to take up his power, find his center of self-control,
I lost my lover to his need to stay a child,

and the spell was broken.

Magician

It was the kind of trick
you've seen before,

where the magician
allows the audience
to believe they understand

exactly how the magic
is done, right until
his last reveal,

when it becomes clear,
that is not at all
how he did it.

Your surprise clouds
every other possibility,
creating the usual mystery,

like he's done with you
so many times before, but
you still don't see it coming.

That's how he made me
stay with him so long.

Spilling Away

Wine spilled, covered the books.
Floor still sticky, dirty sticky,
like nobody ever cleaned it up,
but I did, right away.

Mess of a love affair ending now.
Spilled like wine, sticky and stained,
like nobody tried to make it better,
but I did, and I did, and I did.

One of us hides like a bandit,
and one of us lives in a fantasy.
Sometimes we swap and it almost works,
until we spill out in such a sticky mess.

How might we keep our love
from spilling away forever?

Unpacking a Year

I have taken away all of it, down to
the last little bit of me in your house.

Slowly over a year my small comforts
crept into your space with me.

It took a year to get close, near enough
to see your pain, but not to ease it.

Our time together was insufficient
to find solid footing for a path together.

My overnight bag is tucked away.
Something feels oddly out of place.

Just one thing missing, I can see.
My joy must be there with you.

Separating the Bleeding Things

> "She who loves must also learn
> how to organize pain."
> —Latorial Faison

She finds ways to file away awful hurt,
to deal with it some other day.

Her heart and mind ache from the bruising
of unrecognized trauma, but, no time for angst,

she separates bleeding things into I-can-help
and not-me/not-now.

The latest scar-maker enters, expecting
her solace, but finds only

her lessons-learned triage system.

Strength of a Wish

Sometimes a wish
is not a failure,

but seeps its way deep
into a purple heart,

shovels a tunnel
into a crusted mind,

until it cannot be
forgotten, only released

like a hopeful prayer
winging softly away,

carrying a lover's song
toward no one there.

Meet for Coffee

"I could never be with anyone
who doesn't drink coffee black,"
he once posted.

"I like dishevelment.
In fact, I don't trust places
that are too neat," he stated.

Stuck with me, clearly.

Now he wants to meet for coffee,
and see the place where I live.
He'll find out soon enough.

Walls

Sometimes a flashing memory of you
flies like an arrow with a love note,

arcing over the flowering garden wall
I have built around my heart.

Unbidden, your blue-hazel eyes appear,
smiling out of an artful rendering

of someone who is not at all you,
hanging in a house that is not mine.

It's the saddest mystery I know of,
that two people who love so deeply

cannot find a way to take down
the walls separating them.

Prisoner

Staring at your photo with the top hat and sunglasses,
I am immobilized, unbelieving, as though
you have been listed among the missing-in-action,
and I don't know if you're doing okay.

Will you be found dead, or returned to me alive?
Will you be the same one who kissed me a hungry
good-bye with longing in your eyes? Or will some
awful fear numb you to every sweet thing in life?

Longing to hear your voice say something, anything,
I play your old phone messages over and over,
but no new words of love are there, and hearing
your voice cracks my heart a little each time I listen.

But you are not missing at all, my beloved.
You are choosing not to be with me, ever again.
Breathless tears and piercing longing will not bring
you back from wherever you are tightly locked away.

Even when you are not with me, you are here, warm,
patchouli-scented and palpable, and now I don't know
if I'm doing okay. It's becoming clear to me that
I am the Prisoner.

Casting Stones

To those who would stone me
because you believe you are righteous
and I am not—

I ask you to search your mind
for some deep need, a hungry desire
beyond your rightful reaching,

Then see my own thirst in fresh light,
new understanding, also connecting
to the holy, and stone me not.

Go home to your lives in peace.

I Don't Even Ask

Am I now so jaded, so broken by failure,
betrayal and heartbreak, that I no longer
look at the reality of a man, just toss him
without clarification?

Sixty-three and unmarried? That one's bound
to have awful habits, sad moods, family secrets,
or absolutely no sense about his own money.
I don't even ask their stories anymore.

No, I don't like that about me,
but there it is.

Count the Stars

"Please . . . to hear your lovely voice . . .
a simple conversation," your note asks, because
you have not yet heard me speak.

>No, I don't want to hear your voice if there's
>no way we'll ever be anything more than
>pen pals. Imagining your voice will do.

"We shall count the stars out loud," you write poetically,
though they'll be seen from our two cities, far apart.

>No, I don't want to hear you speak my name,
>because your voice will echo in my memory later,
>rattling in my hollow hours, words said and unsaid
>scrambling together with feelings.

"Be the yang to my yin, the yin to my yang,"
you suggest. Living apart, how could we find
such a flow of being?

>No, speaking to each other directly is for people
>who expect to have some future together, or
>at least know that the real-life present moment
>is theirs to share honestly.

"How might we know these simple pleasures
in spite of the distance between us?"

>"Write to me of the stars," I reply.

Did You Notice?

Did you notice?

That I wore my most flattering color today,
that my earrings matched my blouse,
both chosen to please you?

That I could not turn my eyes from you,
noticing still-strong legs, capable hands,
your favorite cap pulled from your Mustang?

That I let you stand a little too close, turned
toward you, doe-eyed, as you spoke to me,
your words almost like you still loved me?

Searching Remembered Rooms

Free of myself, I wandered remembered rooms,
full of people I knew or loved, or still love, amazed
to find them there, jamming together in a house I

once owned, or maybe two houses, morphed for vague
subject matter relevance, until there was just one house
with blended purposes and memories all mashed up until I

could not decipher persons or the ways I had known them.
Nor did it matter that I could not, for everyone was happy
to be playing music together. Noticing your absence, I

floated through all the rooms, the yard, to the river's edge,
searching for you, my long ago music man. Accepting
that you weren't coming, sad-but-angry tears woke me.

Companionship

Why would I ever give up
the free reins of the life
I have in widowhood?

Indeed, it is my first
solo experience
living in real freedom,

    having, doing and being
    everything I desire,

missing only the everyday sharing
of a good life in unbridled passion
with one true companion.

Spending My One Life

Some days I just have to pull back,
stop reviewing my past lovers,
those poorly thought-out candidates
curiously judged worthy in the moment.

Else, my today drains away, washed
over by flooding sorrow, stinking regret
that this one or another could not be
the right one for more than a little while.

It's a lesson not a lifespan, a friend said.
I narrow my focus to today as I decide
how to spend my one life.

The First One After

Too young not to love again after my spouse's death,
I imagined a résumé for the first one after.
He would be a musical, energetic, funny,
generous, brilliant, attractive person.
Working on the list drew me out of my grief.

Can I feel the same joy in partnering
as in that last marriage? Am I being selfish
or short-sighted to hold out for the same affection?
I have grown since his passing and wonder
whether a new lover might fit me even better.

Yes, the next love will have its own passions,
distinct differences, unique to the pairing,
which we will come to crave, and then wonder
how we managed without the other.
Seeking actively, this shouldn't take long, right?

Ten years passed quickly. The first, second and third
lovers have come and gone, each with desired qualities,
but I had not thought to list stability and moderation,
emotional availability and honesty. Now only
my ever-longer partner preference list remains.

Love Is

Love is
a drunken dance where
everyone laughs
and no one leads.

Love is
wrapping her up, top to bottom,
in three blankets in your drafty house,
because she is precious to you.

Love is
moonlight over the kitchen sink,
shining on nearly naked bodies,
sharing heavenly-light kisses.

Love is
soups and stews in take-with-you jars
to warm a not-really-lonely man's
solitary dinner time.

Love is
Niagara's exciting thunder, refreshing mist,
treacherous whirlpooling waters,
the ruinous rocks of a black shoreline.

Love is
hurrying unbreathing to the lover's side,
as ambulances rush to the scene
of a five-car crash, imagining life without him.

Love is
one hand reaching out in the night
to be sure the other is there,
and the lover's hand squeezing back.

Just Once More

I have had my salty sunrises at the beach,
blushing pink, with a lover's hand in mine;

Witnessed canyon-red sunsets
with a lover who took my breath away;

Breathed in sync, as we relaxed into the fullness
of August's rosy moon above a roiling ocean;

Kissed the one I love as we lay shivering on a blanket
under icy-blue December's shooting stars;

Hunkered down with my mate as a hurricane danced
in darkness above our heads, washing away our yard;

Howled alone through the last ten full Wolf Moons,
that my voice might be heard by just one more mate.

About the Author

Pamela's poems have been published in the *Virginia Bards Central Review, Virginia Writers Club Journal, Wingless Dreamer, Poetry Society of Virginia Journal, Vallum, Barstow & Grand V, MindFull Magazine, Dark Moon Magazine,* and in several volumes of international collections published by *The Poet Magazine*. Several of her individual poems and collections have received honors in contests.

Pamela's chapbook, *Renewal* (upon which her collection *The Right Mistakes* is based), received an Honorable Mention in a 2020 National Poetry Writing Month Contest. In 2019 Pamela won the Hampton Roads Writers Conference Poetry Contest with her poem "Mrs. Creekmore's May Peas," about the mass shooting in Virginia Beach. *The Right Mistakes* was published by Kelsay Books in 2022.

Pamela's career-based writing included contract nonfiction, instructional design and manuals, developmental and copy editing, and online/print writing for her regional newspaper and internet gateway. She is also a musician and singer and has worked professionally in that arena, too. A mother and grandmother, Pamela resides in eastern Virginia but travels all she can.

Artist's Statement

Retired now, I am harvesting forty years of poetry, songwriting, journals and travelogues to create new works—and fun! I am inspired by the natural world and all sorts of creative arts. The brevity of form in poetry is the most immediately accessible type of art when that inspiration comes to me. A daily writer for a very long time, my affirmation is "May I never cease to be amazed!"

www.ingramcontent.com/pod-product-compliance
Lightning Source LLC
Chambersburg PA
CBHW070939160426
43193CB00011B/1738